WHAT'S IN YOUR MACARONI AND CHEESE?

Jaclyn Sullivan

PowerKiDS press

New York

To cheesy chicks, Tiff and Jamie

Published in 2012 by The Rosen Publishing Group, Inc.
29 East 21st Street, New York, NY 10010

First Edition

Editor: Sara Antill
Book Design: Greg Tucker

Photo Credits: Cover, pp. 8 (left), 8–9, 10, 11 (top, bottom), 13, 14, 15 (bottom), 20 Shutterstock.com; p. 4 BananaStock/Thinkstock; p. 5 Stockbyte/Thinkstock; p. 6 Hans Wild/Time & Life Pictures/Getty Images; p. 7 (top) Herbert Orth/Time & Life Pictures/Getty Images; p. 7 (bottom) Jim R. Bounds/Bloomberg/Getty Images; p. 12 Jupiterimages/Creatas/Thinkstock; pp. 15 (top), 22 Yellow Dog Productions/The Image Bank/Getty Images; p. 16 Tom Grill/Getty Images; p. 17 Jupiterimages/Polka Dot/Thinkstock; p. 19 Jamie Grill/Getty Images; p. 21 Jochen Sand/Photodisc/Thinkstock.

Library of Congress Cataloging-in-Publication Data

Sullivan, Jaclyn.
 What's in your macaroni and cheese? / by Jaclyn Sullivan. — 1st ed.
    p. cm. — (What's in your fast food)
 ISBN 978-1-4488-6212-2 (library binding) — ISBN 978-1-4488-6383-9 (pbk.) —
ISBN 978-1-4488-6384-6 (6-pack)
 1. Cooking (Pasta)—Juvenile literature. 2. Cooking (Cheese)—Juvenile literature. 3. Nutrition—Juvenile literature. 4. Convenience foods—Juvenile literature. I. Title.
 TX809.M17S94 2012
 641.82'2—dc23
                                                2011032104

Manufactured in the United States of America

CPSIA Compliance Information: Batch #WW12PK: For Further Information contact Rosen Publishing, New York, New York at 1-800-237-9932

Contents

These boys are using a lot of energy playing soccer. Our bodies get energy from the food we eat.

You may think you know what is in macaroni and cheese. After all, it is all in the name, right? However, the macaroni and cheese that you make from a box has much more in it than just cheese and macaroni. Some of these things are good for you. Others may not be very healthy for your body. This book will help you figure out which is which!

Macaroni and cheese is such a popular food that

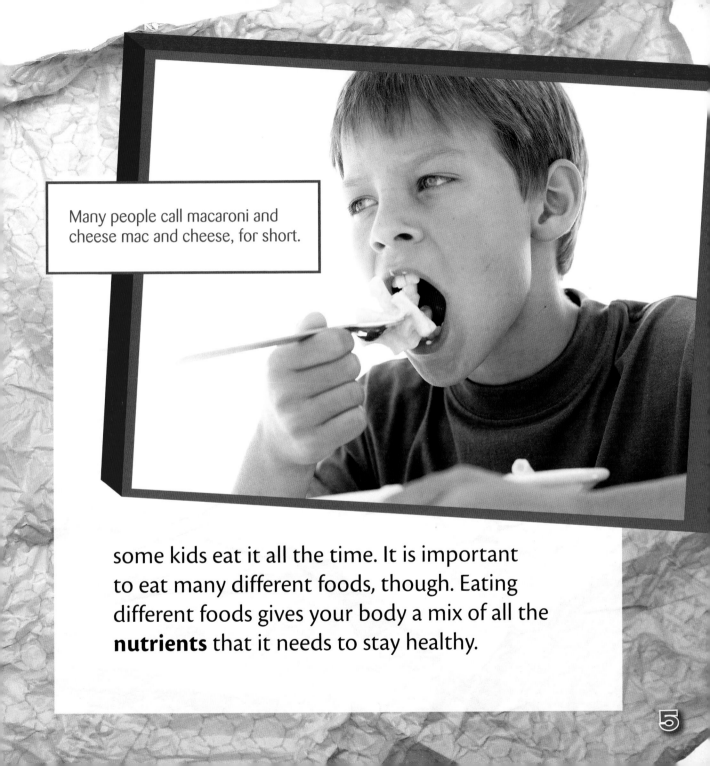

Many people call macaroni and cheese mac and cheese, for short.

some kids eat it all the time. It is important to eat many different foods, though. Eating different foods gives your body a mix of all the **nutrients** that it needs to stay healthy.

The Blue Box

In the United States, macaroni and cheese has been around in some form for over 200 years! Many people think it came to the United States with Thomas Jefferson, the third US president. Jefferson first tasted macaroni and cheese in Europe. He enjoyed it so much that he served it at the White House!

This family is eating dinner together in 1943. Meat and dairy products were hard to get during World War II, which lasted from 1939 until 1945.

Today, most people recognize the blue box of macaroni and cheese sold by Kraft Foods. Kraft's boxed macaroni and cheese was first sold in 1937. It became very popular during World War II when people were looking for foods without meat in them.

Thomas Jefferson was the president of the United States from 1801 until 1809. His 1787 drawing of a pasta machine is held at the Library of Congress, in Washington, D.C.

FAST-FOOD FACTS

Kraft sells around 350 million boxes of macaroni and cheese every year in the United States. Its macaroni and cheese is also very popular in other countries.

Making Macaroni and Cheese

When macaroni and cheese is made from scratch, it usually has four main **ingredients**, or parts. As you might guess, the first ingredient is macaroni. Macaroni is a type of pasta. The second ingredient is cheese. The third and fourth ingredients are butter and milk. Cheese, butter, and milk are all **dairy** products. Dairy products come from animals like cows and goats!

Macaroni and cheese can be made on the stove, as this woman is doing, or baked in an oven. Some kinds can even be made in a microwave.

People make macaroni and cheese in different ways. Some people put extra things, like broccoli or hot dogs, in their macaroni and cheese. Others use different shapes of pasta instead of macaroni. Some even use spaghetti!

Cheese and butter are both made from the milk of animals such as cows.

Pasta

Pasta, the first ingredient in macaroni and cheese, is made from durum wheat. A part of the wheat called **semolina** is mixed with water and sometimes eggs. This creates pasta **dough**. The pasta dough is kneaded, or pressed, to make it stronger. The dough is then pushed through machines that cut it into different shapes, like elbow macaroni or spaghetti.

Durum wheat is a hard type of wheat. Flour made from hard wheat can be used to make pasta and some kinds of bread.

Once pasta is cut, it goes through a dryer. The dryer, like a blow dryer you might use on your hair, blows hot air on the pasta to dry it out. The pasta is then packaged and sent to stores and restaurants.

This pasta dough is being rolled flat. It can then be cut into different shapes.

FAST-FOOD FACTS

Pasta comes in many shapes. Farfalle is also called bow tie pasta because it is shaped like a bow tie! Pasta shaped like a shell is called conchiglie. Fusilli is a spiral-shaped pasta.

The Big Cheese

This boy is drinking a glass of milk. Like cheese, milk has a lot of calcium in it.

Cheese is the other main ingredient in macaroni and cheese. Different types of cheeses are made all around the world. These cheeses all have different flavors. The most common cheese used in macaroni and cheese is cheddar. Cheddar can be white, yellow, or orange.

Cheese has **calcium**, which helps keep your bones strong. It also has protein, which helps your muscles stay strong. Cheese

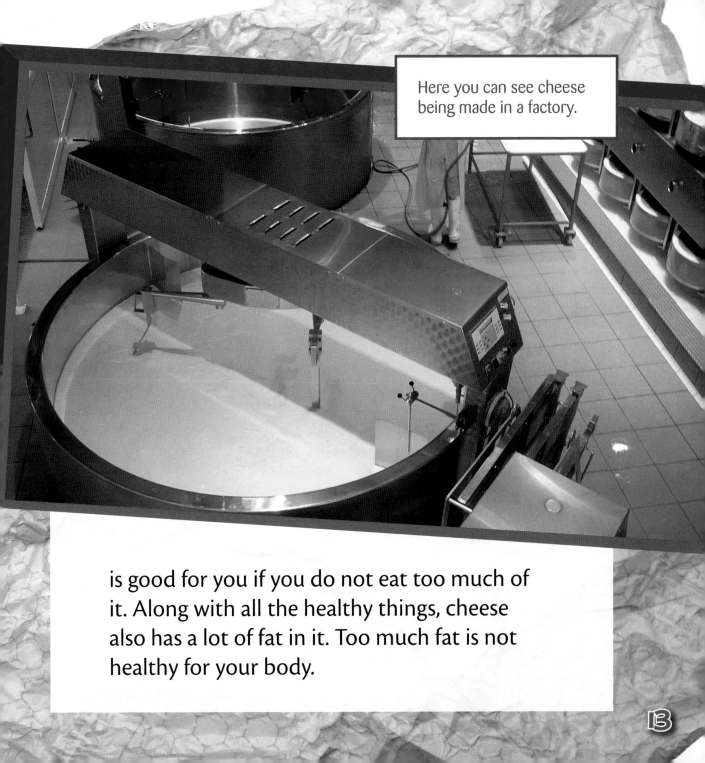

Here you can see cheese being made in a factory.

is good for you if you do not eat too much of it. Along with all the healthy things, cheese also has a lot of fat in it. Too much fat is not healthy for your body.

Cheese Powder

If you have ever watched an adult make macaroni and cheese from a box, you have probably seen a packet of orange powder or sauce go into the pot. This is a cheese-like product called **processed** cheese.

To make processed cheese, real cheese is melted and mixed with water and salt. **Artificial**, or man-made, flavors

Homemade macaroni and cheese is often a pale yellow color, unlike the bright yellow and orange of boxed macaroni and cheese. This is because of the different types of cheese used.

and colors are added. These colors and flavors make the processed cheese look and taste more like real cheese. Processed cheese is cheaper to use than real cheese and lasts longer. However, processed cheese goes through many changes that add unhealthy things to it.

Adding a piece of fruit and a carton of milk to your school lunch is a great way to get nutrients that your body needs.

FAST-FOOD FACTS

The most popular type of processed cheese in the United States is American cheese. It is often used in grilled cheese sandwiches and cheeseburgers.

Fat and Sodium

Your doctor measures your height and weight at your yearly checkup. She can tell you if you have a healthy amount of fat in your body.

Many of the ingredients used to make macaroni and cheese have fat in them. That fat can add up when all the ingredients are used together to make macaroni and cheese. Some fat is good for your body. However, extra fat can make your heart work too hard moving blood through your body.

Processed macaroni and cheese has a lot of added **sodium**, too. Too much sodium causes pressure on the veins that move

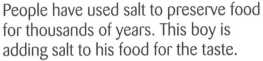
People have used salt to preserve food for thousands of years. This boy is adding salt to his food for the taste.

blood in our bodies. Sodium is found in salt. It acts as a **preservative** in food. Boxes of macaroni and cheese can sit on a grocery-store shelf for months. Preservatives keep food from spoiling, or going bad.

Nutrition Facts

Serving Size 1 cup (228g)
Servings Per Container: 2

Amount Per Serving

Calories 250   Calories from Fat 110

	% Daily Value *
Total Fat 12g	18%
Saturated Fat 3g	15%
Trans Fat 0g	
Cholesterol 30mg	10%
Sodium 470mg	20%
Potassium 700 mg	20%
Total Carbohydrate 31g	10%
Dietary Fiber 0g	0%
Sugar 5g	
Protein 5g	10%

Vitamin A 4%	•	Vitamin C 2%
Calcium 20%	•	Iron 4%

*Percent Daily Values are based on a 2,000 calorie diet. Your daily values may be higher or lower depending on your calorie needs.

	Calories	2,000	2,500
Total Fat	Less than	65g	80g
Sat Fat	Less than	20g	25g
Cholesterol	Less than	300mg	300mg
Sodium	Less than	300mg	300mg
Total Carbohydrate		300g	375g
Dietary Fiber		25g	30g

Calories per gram:
Fat 9   •   Carbohydrate 4   •   Protein 4

Macaroni and cheese has a lot of **calories**. Calories are a measure of the energy in the foods we eat. We need to eat a certain number of calories each day to be healthy. When we eat too many calories, though, our bodies store the extra energy as fat.

To find out how many calories are in a box of macaroni and cheese, check the label. Labels

This is an example of a label on a box of macaroni and cheese. The numbers listed are for one serving. If a box has two servings in it and you eat the whole box, you would need to double the numbers.

Comparing the labels on two different boxes of food can help you decide which is healthier.

tell you how many calories and how much fat and sodium come in your box of macaroni and cheese. A label also tells you if there are any healthy things in your macaroni and cheese, like calcium.

Just Add Veggies

This family is eating spaghetti and tomato sauce. Tomatoes have vitamin C, which helps your body fight off illnesses.

Adding vegetables to your macaroni and cheese is a great way to make your meal healthier. Vegetables have nutrients and **vitamins** that keep our bodies working the way they should. Many people like to add broccoli to their macaroni and cheese. Cauliflower, spinach, and peas are great choices, too!

If you are making homemade macaroni and cheese, you could

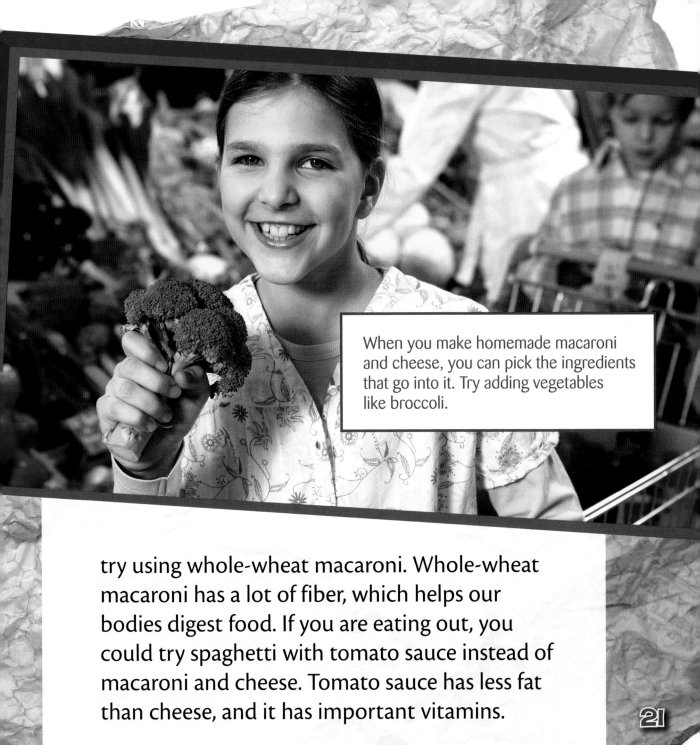

When you make homemade macaroni and cheese, you can pick the ingredients that go into it. Try adding vegetables like broccoli.

try using whole-wheat macaroni. Whole-wheat macaroni has a lot of fiber, which helps our bodies digest food. If you are eating out, you could try spaghetti with tomato sauce instead of macaroni and cheese. Tomato sauce has less fat than cheese, and it has important vitamins.

Be Smart

Eating a healthy lunch will give you the energy you need to feel good for the rest of the afternoon.

It is important to make good choices about the food you eat whenever you can. Talk to your parents about making macaroni and cheese at home with real cheese and vegetables. When you eat out at a restaurant or at school, remember that tomato sauce is usually healthier than processed cheese sauce.

Your body will work best when you give it healthy food. Take care of your body because you get only one!

Glossary

artificial (ar-tih-FIH-shul) Made by people, not nature.

calcium (KAL-see-um) An element found in nature. It is needed for strong bones and teeth.

calories (KA-luh-reez) Amounts of food that the body uses to keep working.

dairy (DER-ee) Having to do with foods, such as cheese, that are made from milk.

dough (DOH) A thick mix from which food is made.

ingredients (in-GREE-dee-unts) The different things that go into food.

nutrients (NOO-tree-ents) Food that a living thing needs to live and grow.

preservative (prih-ZER-vuh-tiv) A substance that keeps something from going bad.

processed (PRAH-sesd) Something that is treated or changed using a special series of steps.

semolina (seh-muh-LEE-nuh) A part of durum wheat used to make pasta.

sodium (SOH-dee-um) An element found in nature.

vitamins (VY-tuh-minz) Nutrients to help the body fight illness and grow strong.

Index

Web Sites

Due to the changing nature of Internet links, PowerKids Press has developed an online list of Web sites related to the subject of this book. This site is updated regularly. Please use this link to access the list:

www.powerkidslinks.com/food/cheese/